MW01241815

My First Journey to America:

to America:

My Most Fascinating Episodes
A memoir

August 1962

By
Sifas Eliphas Zhou

My First Journey to America:

My Most Fascinating Episodes
A memoir

Copyright © September, 2021 by Sifas
Eliphas. Zhou.

ISBN: 9798472239899
Category: Non Fiction, Autobiography
Library of Congress Cataloging-in-Publication
Data

Printed in the United States of America

DEDICATION

These memories are dedicated to:

My loving wife **Sophia**

My dearest children:
"Doc" Natsai & Dan
Ratie
Tinei
"Bee" Batie
Vushe & "Mamthembu" Mveli
Zenzo & Leanne
Kwane & Simba

My adorable
granddaughters: & grandsons:

Tiana	**"Jr" Sheu**
Chichi	**Chris**
Nana	**Khanya**
Shyloh	**Anesu**
Ari	**Yanga**
Lolo	**Nyasha**
Elianna	

My sweetest great-granddaughter:
Noe

Acknowledgement:

My beloved Zhou Family,

I want to thank two incidents which persuaded me to retrieve this six-decade old tale from the dusty archives of time in order to share it with you before the sun sets on my life.

First was the sight of Life-Jackets which you see worn by Doc, and Bee on their unforgettable Mexican holiday wit Ratie, posted on *Zviri mu Mhuri* WhatsApp forum. If anything ever evoked the deepest Nostalgia [a longing for things past and experiences] in me, it was that sight. Those Life-Jackets brought back memories of me wearing a similar attire on board an Ocean Liner, the DE BEERS during my first JOURNEY TO AMERICA in August 1962.

An overnight flight took me from Salisbury to Charles de Gaul International in Paris. I stayed in Paris for 3 weeks before embarking on a 9 day sail to the New York. With me were 3 000 other students who on arrival lined up to wave back to the Majestic Stature of Liberty which, in the sea which seemed to wave a Welcoming gesture to the incoming guests. It had been a turbulent time sailing on the stormy North Atlantic Ocean from Le Havre in France to New York Harbor in the United States.

Second, because it was my fault that I let the cat out of the bag that by triggering the second incident, accidentally by mentioning to two of our indefatigable *varoora*;" Mamthembu" Mveli and Leann. The two are the sort of women who knew an adventure when they saw one. An uncanny happenstance had happened in their view. The two seemed to have connived with each other in order to persuade me to retrieve the story from the Archives of time, dusty it, and put it in black and white.

Uncanny because the two, as you know, live worlds apart. Mveli in Canada and Leann in Cape Town, at the time. So how did they insist on the same thing? And who was I to resist?

I consented, and the result is what you are about to read. Many thanks to Babamunini Tinashe Nhongo, who helped with the transcription of this memoir, and "Doc" Natsai for the edits and final touches.

But before you read it there remains a vital question:
For what purpose was I embarking on such a risky Journey - Christopher Columbus's style?
The answer is what follows.

Sometime in the early 60's - the dying days of an ambitious experiment called 'THE FEDERATION OF RHODESIA AND NYASALAND' - there suddenly opened up a floodgate of opportunities, hitherto unavailable to African students to advance their education beyond secondary school to university level.

Unsurprisingly the floodgate was not opened by the Rhodesian racist regime. It was opened by sympathetic foreign governments, namely; America, Europe, Canada, Australia, New Zealand, even the Soviet Union, including

Ghana and Sierra Leone.

However, the only way a student could access those opportunities was though a scholarship; and *I happen to be one of those who won it.*

In fact I was one of THREE students [see Bios p.] who pioneered the exodus from our Church - the Evangelical Lutheran Church in Rhodesia [ELCR]. The other two were Thomas Tlou and Mushori Zhou.

While Thomas was awarded an uncontested scholarship by the Lutheran World Federation [LWF] to study at Luther College, Decorah, Iowa, (1962), Mushori and I had to battle it out against hundreds, if not, thousands of other aspiring students throughout the Federation, screened though SAT (Scholarstic Aptitude Test) and rigorous interviews for the coveted *African Scholarship Programme Of American Universities* [ASPAU]. This was an initiative of President J.F. Kennedy, himself, during the Cold War in order to uplift blacks.

Eventually Mushori got admitted at *Missouri University* Missouri State (1961), and I at *Wittenberg University*, Springfield, Ohio (1962).

As can be expected, Mushori and I had harrowing albeit, different stories to tell. Let mine be for another day.

But for now, I have cherry-picked some *EPISODES WHICH FASCINATED ME GREATLY* during that historic journey.

It was a journey that began in the backwoods of Nyamhondo Chief's area, Belingwe (Mberengwa) district and ended in the green hills of tall pine forests of *Warren Pennsylvania*, North America. [*see NOTE 3*].

The EPISODES are a synthesis of what has remained indelibly engraved in my memory for all those 60 odd years - or almost.

Your loving Dad and Grandpa

SHOKA FARM – GWANDA
April 2020

THE EPISODES

The episodes are the story. The first episode are how the story began; the last is how it ended.

All taken, they neatly fall into FIVE SECTIONS, namely:

SECTION ONE

EPISODE 1. From home to Salisbury Airport

"Who shall accompany me to Salisbury Airport?" appears a mundane question today. But it loomed high on my parent's minds and agonised them to the end of the earth. Yet I did not see it in a crisis mode as they did. For four years (1955-58) I had been passing through Salisbury while learning at Goromonzi. Salisbury had, therefore, become my stomping ground. Notwithstanding that my father knew that I had not been passing via the Airport. What he knew was that I had no knowledge of the laws of the country. How could I when I had been raised in the rural backwoods of Nyamhondo Chief's Area, herding cattle? Being a law-abiding man, one law of the country he knew had been passed down from the days of Cecil John Rhodes was called *TRESPASSING*. Its consequences were dire. The white racist regimes allowed whites to SHOOT-ON-SIGHT any blacks they found loitering in premises they had no business to transact. And that was the source of his agony.

Accompanying me to the airport was therefore a task my father trusted nobody but himself. But then his health was the fly in the ointment. He was bed-ridden since I ever knew him as a child.

Someone, then suggested that my mother, *VaGambiza* should accompany me, *"Ah! ndigodzoka nani?"* She cried (Ah! who will accompany me back?). It's obvious the suggestion was a non-starter. My mother had never been outside her environment *since she was born* (to quote Ratie, her granddaughter).

But allow a digression here.

Twenty one years later (1983) she became, no doubt, the most air-travelled *Gogo in the whole* of Mberengwa and perhaps, beyond. She flew over 20 000 kilometres to and fro Stockholm for my operation. I was operated in Stockholm where I had been posted as Ambassador. Flying was a treat she took to her grave.

Back to their agonising crisis. They finally

compromised and settled on *Phillipson* (my young brother now regrettably late) and Mainini *Tariraira Gambiza* (now widowed) both teenagers in standard six at the time.

Episode 2

Even that still left my father sceptical. To resolve his scepticism, he sat down and wrote a letter begging his cousin, one, I only knew as *Uncle Dixon* living in Mabvuku Township. He begged him to accompany us to the Airport.

I had never met *Uncle Dixon* before - a barrel - chested middle aged man. Very black in complexion, and aloof in attitude. We found him relaxing on a sofa - a quart of Castle lager in his hand. I wasted no time handing him the letter.

He opened it instantly, but started reading it painfully slowly. Our eyes followed him as he took a deep breath before he found his voice;

"*Accompanying you! Where are you flying to?*" he

sniffed.

"To America!" I briskly answered.

"Really? What for?" he enquired cynically.

"To study" I snapped back.

"Who is paying for it?" he sought details with the precision of a tooth pick.

"A scholarship! I won a scholarship!" I emphasized expecting a compliment.

Instead, he mumbled more to himself than to us.

"Ah! Ha-a-a! SAKA PAKAFAMBA TSOTSO KA APA. HANDITI!?" ("Ah! Ha-a-a! So you used African magic here, too. Didn't you?)

I was mortified. And when I was just at the point of rudely asking him what he meant by that an unbidden memory of what my Goromonzi teacher, G.D Mhlanga used to tell us, rescued me.

"You can take an African out of his primitive environment very easily, but cannot easily take that primitive environment out of him!!"

In the end Uncle Dixon did not even bother himself accompanying us to the Airport. He simply ordered a Taxi cab to come and pick us and drop us at a bus terminus somewhere in town. There we boarded a bus bound for the Airport. That was how we got to the Airport.

SECTION TWO:

From Salisbury Airport to Charles De Gaul

We had no hustles finding the desk to check in my only big bag. Thereafter, we navigated our way through a crowd where mothers were hugging their sons fare well, here, and fathers lecturing others, there. I was in a hurry leading my two escorts upstairs to the balcony for two reasons: One was to show them where to stand in order to see me board the plane; the other was to find *a free table* where we would also partake in our *LAST SUPPER*.

Episode 3

I found the table and I remember that *LAST SUPPER* well. I gave a half a dozen cream buns and a bottle of coca cola to each - quite a treat for children never used to eating such large quantities of confectionary at one go. Meanwhile I busied myself studying details of my itinerary. On my side was a cup of hot tea and nothing else.

I cannot deny that I felt like an Astronaut being

accompanied to a launching pad.

A minute later an announcement came on from the public address system:

DOUGLAS DC 6 TO CHARLES DE GAUL NOW BOARDING!; We jumped up.

I remember grabbing both their arms and saying; *"This is the moment we have been waiting for. We now have to part"*

I hugged them emotionally and thanked them dearly. I jogged downstairs and handed my ticket to a British Air ways Official, then my Passport to the Immigration Desk. They simply stamped in it and grudgingly threw it back to me. They ordered me to proceed to the Departure Lounge.

The Departure Lounge, already packed up with departing students had an eerie atmosphere smacking of a place where animals are held in quarantine.

To be in quarantine has never been for a good reason. There lay the cause of my nervousness. This, remember, was my first flight. I looked around wondering who else was nervous. There didn't seem to be any. But if I was going to die, there in the far corner of the Departure Lounge were two familiar faces who were going to die with me: *Quinton Malianga* and *Samson Mahali*. Both were my classmates at Goromonzi four years earlier in 1958. One abiding memory I had of them was their frequent visits to Mr. J.M. Hammond's office every Friday afternoon for flogging. Hammond was our Principal, renowned for strict discipline.

Then I feared; if his flogging had not weaned them from their notoriety, their company on this flight did not augur well for our journey. It was bad news.

"Hello! you two!" I hollered at them.

"Hello Sifi" they answered back in a chorus.

Excitement was high. We embraced and laughed hilariously.

They led the way and I followed them as the queue wound out and then up a ladder leaning at the door of the plane.

Episode 4

I did not forget to look back at the balcony. Indeed! There stood Phillipson and Mainini Tari, at the spot I instructed them to stand waiving at me like mad. I was touched. Beads of tears ran down my cheeks.

My first impression of the inside of the plane was a disappointment. The seats were just like those of a bus except each had a seatbelt, and a sort of board attached at the back to use as a table.

Episode 5

Then my fear that what often happened in buses might happen here was vindicated. A scramble for window seats ensued. Chaos broke out when legitimate owners of those seats demanded them at all costs. They seemed ready for a physical confrontation. Peace was only restored when a member of the crew intervened.

Examining my own ticket closely I was surprised. Seats were clearly numbered and stapled on.

Guess who was instigating the chaos? Quinton and Samson, and yet we had not seen the last of them.

Episode 6

No sooner had the plane gained flight altitude than it lost it again. That hardly took an hour. I certainly thought that was it. It would be end of us. Passengers screamed. Bowels flew up. Heads swivelled.

The Captain's voice, however, quickly came to our relief:

"What you can see below is the Kariba gorge. The largest man-made lake South of the Equator. It is only second to the Aswan Dam in Africa, on the Blue Nile, in Egypt"

Then he added a specious claim: so I thought.
"The two are the only objects you can see from the moon."

Later, I came to learn that one can also see the *Great Wall of China* and even the *Great Dyke of Zimbabwe's* Chrome- rich reef stretching some 300 kilometres.

As soon as the plane regained its flying altitude, the sound of trolleys trouncing the floor was a sign that Supper was ready. The leading trolley carried food. There was a choice of beef, fish, or vegetarian. The second: soft drinks or plain water. I also remember that nips of Whisky, Champaign, or brandy were available for those who paid cash. It was that supper which prompted the *Seventh episode*.

Episode 7

When peoples' stomachs are full, it always seems they seek ways of expending their energies. So were the passengers. Up-and-down, up-and-down, they trekked in the crowded alley in perpetuity. I was nervous. Having never been airborne, I certainly believed that, that sort of commotion could destabilize the plane. I noticed who the leaders were: Quinton and Samson. But then, they suddenly disappeared at the back. I was curious. I unfastened my seatbelt and went to find out. There, they were authoritatively established at the entrance of the toilets marshalling people in and out. Obviously, people objected. Arguments erupted. Nips of whisky and brandy had kicked in. Eyes rolled right and left menacingly. I was one of those who panicked, but seemed to be the only one who feared that the situation might reach a dangerous stage. The Cockpit had to know. So I slipped away and went to give a report. I was back with a member of the crew, only to find the scene of the brawl deserted.

Embarrassed, all I could do was point at the mess: the overflowing ashtrays with cigarette stubs, the wet floors, and worse the offensive smell which somebody said of *mbanje* (daga or marijuana). Surely that was sufficient evidence for him to go on the public address system and admonish the offenders. But he didn't.

Instead, the man looked at me bemused. He must have thought I was crazy because he remarked:

"Look! Fellow! This is the place where people are allowed to smoke!" and banged his knuckles on an ashtray and left.

I was non-plussed. I strongly suspected that his acquiescing to such behaviour was enough proof that he also indulged in them.

A cluster of distant lights twinkling below us suddenly grew into a sea. The Captain's voice came on again informing us that we had reached Brazzaville the Capital of Belgian Congo and not of ZAIRE, now Democratic Republic of Congo (DRC), next door. That was our first stop since we left Salisbury. We were allowed to stretch our legs and disembark. The real reason, however was to allow an army of cleaners to come up and clean the plane. They carried black plastic bags, brooms, and detergents.

Episode 8

"Ho! ho! ho!" passengers moaned. At first I was alarmed thinking they feared that the army of cleaners

would tinker with their brief-cases, but no. In truth it was the sizzling temperatures even after sun set. That was why the work suits of cleaners were baggy khaki shorts or half-trousers reaching just below their knees, worn with their oversized shirts with large short-sleeves.

Episode 9

Talk of cleaning our toilets. But entering their own toilets, the first thing that hit me was the stench. Then I wondered; if they had the enthusiasm of cleaning ours, why not theirs? A few of us who returned to the plane easily witnessed plain fakery. The one cleaner wearing gloves removed the soiled black plastic bags from underneath a wooden cover in the toilet, and tossed it into some sort of portable dust bin. The other carrying fresh black plastic bags simply clipped them on as replacements, a process that took a fraction of the time it takes a mother to change her baby's napkins.

Soon, all passengers were back. Bringing the rear were three or four new faces – ASPAU students – I presumed. It confirmed the rumour that our plane was Chartered to zig-zag around African capitals picking up ASPAU students.

Night had fallen when the plane took off to our second stop, N'Djamena, the Capital of Chad (or Tchad) a former French Colony. We picked up more students but not all passengers witnessed it because they were asleep.

The irredeemable loss on tourism, was however the fantastic scenery of the Sahara Desert over which we flew almost midnight. They say the sand-dunes, dotted with several oases, have a heavenly appearance from the sky.

Our third stop was Tripoli. This ancient sea port is also the capital of Libya commanding international ships on the Mediterranean Sea coming to fetch oil.

Twenty four years later (1986), I would remember Libya as a filthy-rich oil-producing country under its flamboyant leader, Colonel Gadaffi. I had the rare opportunity to shake his effeminate hand popping out of snow-white silk garment at the HICC (Harare International Conference Centre). I was Deputy Secretary for NAM (Non- Aligned Movement) for which he arrived in style. Gadaffi caused a stir when he brought his look-alike and two Mercedes Benz. That way we could not tell in which car he was. In any case, his battalion of female security gave no quarter to ruffians or thugs trying to get close to the Colonel. Their arms were sheathed in long gloves made of sharp spikes that tore into your flesh at a nudge. So a nudge was enough to send crowds helter-skelter, bleeding profusely at the same time. Asked by a journalist how rich Libya was, Gadaffi replied:

"I cannot deny that we are rich."

"I can dole out a million US dollars to each man, woman, and child at the drop of a hat". Which was true.

But as with all autocrats, it was not surprising that his end was ignominious. He fled from his Residence and was captured squatting in a culvert and killed by his own people.

It was well after midnight when we flew over the Mediterranean Sea. Breakfast was served as we flew over Italy, and by 7.00 am, we landed at our final destination – *CHARLES DE GAUL AIRPORT*, in France.

As one of Europe's longest airports, I got the impression that it was also the busiest until I passed through *Frankfurt* in West Germany. There, I witnessed planes taking off and landing every *THREE SECONDS*!

Paris, therefore, was the first city I ever set my foot on the European continent-ending the first leg of my journey to America.

As the plane taxed towards its GATE, I looked outside and saw the *MOTHER OF ALL DIFFERENCES* between the *FIRST* and the *THIRD* world. In the *FIRST WORLD*, to embark or disembark, passengers never walk out to an outdoor flight of stairs like we did in Salisbury. From the plane, they simply step onto an enormous cavernous conduit that automatically shunts onto the door of the plane and come out to find themselves right in the

Baggage Claim area, where they wait for their luggage to be   disgorged   onto   the   conveyor   belt

SECTION THREE:

Three Weeks in Paris

We picked our luggage, cleared the Immigration and Customs formalities, uneventfully. But then we wondered where to go. Someone directed us to a very large Billboard written:

Welcome: ASPAU students

An ASPAU Representative stood by-it holding a bunch of envelops. The star-spangled American Flag was prominently embossed on top of each envelop. Our curiosity was on its contents. Inside was: a cheque (spelt check) pocket money for us to spend. I hastily went to a post office and sent it back home. Then several coupons for:

- food
- lodging;
- local transport by trans;
- entertainment;

and whatever else….I might have forgotten.

It did not take long for us to melt into a convoy of taxis waiting to ferry us to our guest houses for lodging. Little did we know that we were to be French guests for the following three weeks. Weeks during which the two most important pre-occupations were Tourism, and cuisine (EATING). And least did I also know that I was on the verge of running into my next two EPISODES. In retrospect I find it fascinating that while both EPISODES had something to do with Europe, they had more to do with Africa than Europe. So did I have to come all the way to France to discover them, I wondered?

Episode 10

My room-mate. Someone organising our accommodation (in pairs) had used *LANGUAGE* as a criterion. That meant if you spoke English, your room mate would also speak English, French – French, Portuguese – Portuguese, and so on.

"Hello!....", I greeted a guy whose luggage lay at the same door as mine.

"My name is Sifas Zhou, from Belingwe"

"Haro!" he replied. "Mine is Mr. Mbofana from Manicaland, you know. Next to Fort Victoria."

The Concierge (a Hotel staff) gave a key to each of us and left.

We unlocked the room and threw our bags randomly each on a bed nearest to him. We sat down on some sort of sofas on which brochures written in several languages were placed. They were written in English, French, Portuguese, Spanish, Arabic, Chinese, Japanese. After a breezy concentration, we eventually gave up reading. "Hwu-u-u!" my room-mate sighed. *"Jet reg you know jet reg!"*

I looked at him. Quite an innocent and apparently pleasant guy. But how could he shock me speaking English with a Vernacular accent and pronunciation like that? Was he really, an ASPAU, scholar. As I waited when next he opened his mouth, my nerves cringed.

"Wuludu you mind us taking a walk out on the

streets and stretch our regs?" he suggested.

"No! No! No! I wouldn't," I then tried to point out that the word *"Wuludu"* was in fact "Wud", and that the 'l' was silent.

But no! He didn't get it. He continued with could; pronouncing it as 'culudu; 'should' as 'shuludu'; then I knew he was not joking.

Plucking enough courage, I dared asking him whether he was actually a student and to which college he was going. "Oh! Yes! I am a student going to a Seminary- American Methodist Seminary. I will however, have to complete my high school first. That explained it…but still shocked me.

Shocked me because, I did not know that we had schools in Rhodesia which did not bother about English pronunciation. Did I have to come all the way to France to know it? Years later, as Ambassador, (1983), I again had a personal Secretary called Linda. She could not pronounce the word *'sixty'* without a 'k', called it *'sikisiti!!*

Yet against this revelation, fast back, to the 1950's. I remembered two addicts of English pronunciation. One was the Principal of Mnene Boarding School called Obediah Mlilo, and another, Peter Sikakana, my lecturer in P.T.H (Primary Teachers' High) at Musume Teacher Training School. Mlilo would take the whole school to task if he heard only one pupil mispronounced a word. One commonly mispronounced word was 'COMFORTABLE'. A friend of mine, Dwala Dube, who was one of Mlilo's pupils told me that they were made to SING the correct pronunciation the whole 30 minutes they would have been learning something else.

Peter Sikakana, my lecturer from KwaZulu Natal chided us as the "DZE" generation. He told us that we could not pronounce: *"THE"* for instance *"The boy"*. He said we pronounced it as *"Dze boy"*.

So allergic to English mispronunciation were these two eminent educators that one dared not mispronounce a word before them in public for fear of being paraded.

Episode 11

The walk Mbofana suggested took us to one of the most popular tourist attractions in Paris called the *EIFFEL TOWER*. There was an inscription *"Designed by a French Civil Engineer called Alexandre Gustave Eiffel (1832-1923)"*.

First, we circled around it admiring the exquisite art work on all its four sides. Then we decided to sit down on a concrete slab. All that time, we were not aware that we were being photographed.

While we sat down we happened to be expressing a wish that it would have been nice if one of us had a camera. We would take pictures and send them home.

All of a sudden, a hand shot between our heads

holding a camera-one of those instant cameras

called Kodak. Naturally we were shocked, moreso as we did not recognise the face even if it was black. And before we reacted, I was sure the man expected a gust of hostility so he greeted us politely.

"Bon jour, Messieurs!" to which he received a blank reply from us. I remember us looking at each other, confused.

"What are you saying?" Mbofana asked.

"Nou! Nou!"

Then he turned to his Instant Camera, and started scrolling back some pictures he had taken of us. Did we want copies? He enquired. He would give us as many as we wanted for a FRANK each.

Only then did we realise there were people who made a living on that sort of profession-called 'PAPARAZI'. One is lucky if he was not photographed in a compromising situation.

Episode 12

Then came the shocker.

"Which country do you come from? I asked.

"Country? France of course!" pointing his fore finger on the ground to emphasize the country.

"No! I mean the original country, somewhere in Africa" I said.

"Africa? Oh you think, because I am black. I am French. I was born here!"

End of questions.

Fast back, once more to 1958. The Rev. Ndavaningi Sithole wrote a trail-blazing book called *'African Nationalism'*. What dawned on me was his description of two kinds of Colonialism.

One was French. It was known as 'ASSIMILADO'. Once a black man was 'assimilated' he said, he would have to be everything 'French' despite his colour. Meaning his *language*, his *name*, his *culture*, his *religion*, which was normally Catholic, even his *residence*.

Another was British. As summed up by Cecil John Rhodes, one of the three British Empires he said here were 'EQUAL RIGHTS FOR ALL CIVILISED MEN! [PERSONS]'. But then delegated the power to judge who is *'civilised'* and who is not to the British. The result was that blacks would never pass the test of being *'civilized'* because the British kept on changing goal posts.

As one day followed another, we soon discovered that tourist attractions were also the hunting grounds of "Paparazi". So we decided to avoid them. We therefore decided to spend our time closeted in restaurants or Coffee Cafès.

Episode 13

We had not noticed that in trams, buses, and on bicycles people kept one or two 'sticks' tucked under their armpits.

"What are those? ...those things which stick out of their armpits?" Mbofana asked.

"*Ah! Those?*" I think we must find out.

"*Bon jour! Mademoiselle*", then pointing at the "stick".

The girl on the other side of the counter simply swept it out of the basket from where several of them suck out, and then asked for money. I gave her.

"*Merci!*" I said

"*Merci!*"

Ah, it smells like bread.

"*est brod*" she said.

Strange that they carry bread under their armpits.

Episode 14

Then on one occasion we got into a restaurant and we got shown to a table. There was always a bottle of wine - French wine and a side plate of buns. We sat down and started studying the menu.

I remembered how France is really regarded as having the best cuisine in the world. Most of its dishes are not only familiar, but international viz the French fries, French toast. And so forth.

But then I selected beef ah-la-carte. Mbofana chose the same and we waited.

Eventually, the mouth-watering dishes came. As we started eating, a horrible thought struck me. I had forgotten my wallet. I say "I" because Mbofana always moved without his.

"How shall we pay? I have forgotten my wallet". He said nothing because he had become so depended on me.

The waiter brought us that final menu for us to pick the sweets. We took it and even continued to choose which sweets.

Finally, the waiter brought the bill. We looked at it as if we meant to pay. Then I said *"Sorry we have forgotten our wallets"*. She took back the bill and left. Back came a senior man who asked us to the back of the restaurant. We were asked to take off our clothes and put on the work suits and start washing dishes. Therein started the reparation.

What a finale to have to wash dishes on our last day in Paris. We left what felt like imprisonment quite sober.

We were rushing in to prepare for our departure the following day.

SECTION 4

Day 1

From Le Harve (France) to New York Harbor (USA) aboard the De Beers

"Have you realized that the Americans are obsessed with BIG SIZES?" asked Mbofana.

"From the BIGGEST hamburger to the TALLEST building in the world; the Empire State Building. If it is American, it has got to be the BIGGEST, the TALLEST, and the BEST" he emphasized. Indeed, we were about to witness the Mother of All Welcomes.

EPISODE 15

First Parade

Le Harve Sea port was a hive of activity that day. It featured an enormous dance troupe, the Syncopanted Ladies. These were girls who had come from America to meet us in Paris and then go back with us giving us orientation on American life.

Dressed in white short skirts, red barrettes and white tennis shoes, the Syncopanted Ladies numbered close to 1000. They paraded in front of our ship, a multi-storied painted white as snow. It had two flags flapping merrily atop- one American and another DE BEERS. Large letters on its side attesting the same. The girls stood in dead silence until sound of music from the band. Then suddenly they broke their silence, marching and singing and dancing, flipping their placards like peacocks, now red now white as they marched round and round on the arena.

The first act they put was the American Anthem. The message was clear. They formed a formation of 50 stars on a blue background representing the 50 American states. The second was a bedazzling spectacle of human formation. They marched forming a pattern of large letters, the red side of the placard reflecting the words.

WELCOME TO AMERICA!!

(to a thunderous round of applause!!!!!!)
We were then allowed into the ship, past a man

who distributed handouts bearing information we needed: the number of our bunker, the time table and the entertainments.

A large notice board clearly flickered the weather report, but we ignored it. It said "Windy and overcast" days ahead.

Episode 16
Second Parade

Unless you look through a sort of window, you would not tell the ship had started moving. It's not a train which you can tell, nor a plane. It quietly and imperceptibly slides away. Then the shores begin to get farther and farther away, the jagged horizon of skyscrapers defining the distance.

We crossed the English Channel in a direction those who missed a lesson on the Great Geographic Arch would be totally confused. We seemed to be going to either Canada or Greenland. All in all, the sailing seemed the most peaceful thing yet until we heard a voice calling *"out, out out*!!!"

We ran out of our bunkers into an already crowded alley full of other students stampeding to the decks. Once there, we stood in ordered fashion listening to a man in front of us on a raised platform.

"This is a LIFE JACKET" he held it like a salesman in a shop.

"You will need it in times of emergency to save your life|" he continued.

"And this is how you use it," he had a dummy on which he put on the LIFE JACKET. Now he was to demonstrate it by throwing the dummy into a little boat floating down there at the bottom of the ship. *"Tshubwi"* went the dummy , missing the little boat.

The dummy was not supposed to miss the boat. *"You are supposed to jump into the boat and float until someone comes to your rescue"*

These LIFE JACKETS worn by Dr .N Chidavaenzi and Batie Griffin, on their unforgettable holiday are what reminded me of My First Journey to America, the subject of my story. (Back to Zviri muMhuri forum)

We went back to our bunkers with mixed feelings about our safety.

We began to look through our handout. Tomorrow which was our second day, was Africa Day. So we began to plan what to showcase. The other days which followed had no real use for us, to attend or not attend.

The list of entertainments had some interest as Mbofana was keen to know what goes on in films overseas.

Day Two:
Africa Day

The following day still proved us right. The weather was so beautiful that a holiday maker would pay his last coin for it. The air was fresh, breezy, and crisp. The last cloud had disappeared from the sky leaving it as blue as the ocean below it.

Passengers too had equally sensed the freshness of the air. They had come out in style. Bikinis, miniskirts and shawls were the dress code.

The ship itself was a lone ranger. It seemed to be a sole object on a vast expense of the ocean. There therefore was possibility of a collision with anything at all.

Episode 17

We had joined the queue for breakfast in the vast dining hall when, lo and behold, we found, we had company. He introduced himself as Jack Trembek and he had a conversation going with Mbofana in which he introduced his partner as Stephen Creek.

We in turn introduced ourselves as Zhou and Dube (Mbofana), surnames which denoted wild animals.

"*Zhou means Elephant and Dube means Zebra*" I explained.

That got him fired. He started asking us some awkward questions.

"*Hey did you come from Southern Rhodesia in South Africa?*"

"*No. South Rhodesia is one country. Southern Africa is another.*" We corrected him.

"*I figure that there are plenty of wild animals roaming around there. Now what do you do with old people when lions come charging?*" I thought for a moment and cooked up an answer completely out of the cuff.

"*Oh ! we tell them to jump into an elevator and up the tree before the lion gets to them.*" He thought for a while and remarked: "*Imagine and elevator on every tree in Africa for that matter*"

We shared a hilarious laugh.

"A hilarious laugh" because it was like a preview to a previous night – Africa Night. The big event night. The mood was electric. Least did we know that Jack and

Stephen were assigned to us to give us orientation. So we were stuck with them the whole day.

After breakfast, they took us out on the deck. It was already full of people playing outdoor games. We got to some playing snooker. Jack asked, '*Do you know this game?*'

"*Yes we do.*"

Then we proceeded to others playing chess and were asked the same question. "*Yes we do, although we never learnt how to play it*"

Then, to some playing baseball. "*Isn't it different from cricket?*

"*No*" I said "*It's different.*" Then to some playing tennis. Again this was familiar.

Then to some who were bowling. This completely new. Then to those who were playing basketball. The second most popular game in America to

American football. That was completely different to our English soccer.

Episode 18

Because it was hot, I proposed to Mbofana that we must try swimming. Our guides suggested that we get some swimming suits.

We approached the office and got our names entered. We paid and were issued with two pairs. We put them on and went to the swimming pool. Suddenly we ran into a problem. Mbofana would not barge.

I said "*Why?*"

"*Aaah! there are girls*" he said.

"*Well, it doesn't matter. Thera are a whole lot of other boys around*" I said

We stood wondering what to do with Mbofana, as one girl superstitiously exposed her breasts and then leaving her chest bare. They were pads and not real BREASTS. We looked at each other. Does it mean that most of the breasts we see on girls are not REAL? They are FAKE.

After lunch, our American hosts left, and a meeting was called upon by Nigerian students. They wanted to make sure that no other traditional dances were performed besides Nigerian High Life!

That put a hold to the South African, Congo, Ghana, Siera Leone and Rhodesian preparations. We decided to hold our own meeting secretly to counter that.

Episode 19

Just to make sure that their instructions were followed, they went door to door warning:

"Fellows! Fellows! Fellows! Make sure don't embarrass us! Don't embarrass us tonight!'

In our secret meeting, we had the popular Rhumba from Congo:

Tamba Maria: Tenderera tenderera x 2

Zvanhasi ndezveduvo: Tenderera x2

Then another by : *The Queen Of Africa,Miriam Makeba*

And another by *South African King Of Jive*, *Majaivana*

Ghana and Siera Leone had a drama.

And southern Rhodesia had *Muchongowoyo*.

Quinton, Samson, Shamuyarira had their traditional dance gear out:

- well sawn bibis of rabits skin, on their waists
- leopard skin across their chest
- shrill sounding gouds on each leg
- a head gear worn by Chibwe Chitedza (Nkomo himself) that was before ZANU was born (8th Aug 1963)

Time came when we were required on the stage. The three slipped behind some Nigerian students. *"Hey ! You , who are you?"* Called out one Nigerian. The three kept quiet pretending not to hear him.

"Heyi ! You three ! Where do you come from?" as he laid his hand on the shoulder of one of them, a fracas developed. *"Hey don't touch me' " Push him out!"* one Nigerian ordered.

"What does he say? What does he say?"

"It does not matter which country (pronounced cundry) *he comes, simply push him."*

End of our attempt to showcase Africa as a whole.

It was Nigerian High Life all night….. a drab bore to the bone.

We left immediately.

Day 3

The American Day

Just as Africa day came to grief because of Nigerian ignorance, so did the Americans Day come to grief of our ignorance of what to do prevent sea- sickness on the ship.

We had been warned and ignore warning. The warning had clearly said … "WINDY AND OVERCAST DAYS AHEAD".

The   sea-sickness tablets were available in a dispensary located at the entrance of the ship. There was therefore, no reason not to see them. And yet we missed them in our hurry to dress up according to the dress code.

The dress code, according to our leader Eno Ekong , was black suit , black shoes, and black bowtie. After putting on my charcoal suit which I had ordered from South Africa, and my well-polished black shoes from the Edworks Rhodesia Ltd. I looked at others. They had version of black suits and black shoes, such that the only white thing were their white shirts, their teeth and the whites of their eyes.

We, then sat facing a bevy of American girls "dressed to kill" said a guy who strode past us. *"To kill who?"* we responded in chorus.

He, just laughed and continued.

And for sure they were long dresses and long legs walking on stilettoes like Secretary bird. The stilettoes were as long as a javelin. They left nothing to choice. Their faces, eyelashes, eyelids bore a heavy paste of makeup. The whole dance hall was filled with different women perfume scents that led everyone's nose along that direction.

Meanwhile the ship's weather indicator signalled "RED" indicating catastrophe to come. Yet our partners, the American girls seemed not to be bothered about it.

The band was ready, the pianist, the trumpeters , the violinist and the conductor were itching to go.

The whole idea was to give us an orientation of American life by a dance called WALTZ.

Episode 20

Ladies and gentlemen readily stood in pairs waiting for the sound of a tune which imitated:

Trampapa tramapapa
Trampapa tramapapa
Trampapa tramapapa

The couples, hand in hand with ladies left hands over their partner's right shoulders, gents with their right hand around the ladies' waists, whirled and twirled slowly, but deliberately. The count of one, two, three, and one two, three was easily to follow.

Then it was our turn. Three gentlemen dashed for it because it seemed easy. But they did not last. They held their mouths instead and moved out of the door .... Vomiting.

The ship tossed up and down and up and down, without making any progress forward. We had hit a storm.

We said our last prayer. St Paul on his journey's and my teacher, John Beck at Goromonzi, in his Geography lessons, he said then , that the Atlantic had horrific currents. The Pacific Ocean was peaceful. The Atlantic currents that wept up North where we came from. But what we faced was here and now …. *Oh Lord help us!*

Episode 21

Suddenly the entire hall was in disavary. The foreign students who held their mouths now held their stomachs in "projectile" vomiting (if you don't know what projectile vomiting is ask President Mnangagwa in his Gwanda experience).

A warning was sent through Public Address System for us to lie down. We followed the instructions that got us crawling back to our bunkers …. clutching our bowties.

End of American day

I lay in my bunker for four days and nearly died of hunger. The fourth day, I heard a knock, a sort of nurse came up, carrying some sort of tablets. *"Oh! Take these! Didn't you know of seasickness?"*

I took a whole dose of three and within an hour, I was well. I was so well that although the ship was still on roller coaster, I began to enjoy it. But there were only two days left.

The music on the Public Address System had changed a s well. It was the days of Elvis Presley, Chubby Checker even Billy Graham and Negro Siritus. From the Europe. Form Europe came the Beatles and ABBA from Sweden.

It takes a whole morning to park a whole ship in its bay.

But lo and behold! The New York Skyline was a jugged mess of sky scrapers. Closer to us, however, was a tall sculpture of a woman, the Statue of Liberty. It seemed to greet every ship that came into the Harbour. We came out nemeses wave back at it. It's really an amazing work of art. It was located in the ocean such that water surrounded it.

End of the Fourth Part of My Journey to America.

SECTION FIVE

From New York City to Warren, Pennsylvania

As we approached the United States, the American skyline welcomed us with pomp and circumstance. The tallest skyline ever attested to the claim that Americans were obsessed with the SIZE and the TALLEST building in the world.

The Statue of Liberty with her raised hand seemed tp respond to the cheers of 3000 students waiving their hands likc mad.

We disembarked.

We were ferried to the one place the American hosts wanted us to go-The Empire State Building for the last act.

The Tour Guide then took over. She lectured us that what were about to embark on was a one in a life time experience. The lift would take us to the 86th floor. The whole building has 102 floors. This majestic building seemed to swayed imperceptibly back and forth in response to the rotation of the earth.

After the tour, I said Goodbye to Mbofana , I had developed a liking for him and he and become part of me all those 9 days. It meant that we would never see each other again until eternity.

But surprise. surprise I received a letter from someone I did not even know. A white man. So did Mbofana. Mine contained instructions of a bus the Greyhound which I would take from New York town called Warren Pennsylvania.

I collected my only luggage, with man, wondering that was all I had from Africa. I said "yes" that's all.

The journey by Greyhound took several hours. I slept and feared I might miss the town. "*Sleep on*" they said. "*We shall wake you up!*" I then slept with confidence that I would not miss my station.

And finally the bus stopped and I was told to disembark it was almost midnight. Three people were waiting for me. A man , a woman and a small boy about four to six years all white. They called themselves The Whitehills. That was my host family.

Episode 22

I was hungry, but they never gave me anything to eat. They just showed me to my bedroom, and bade me goodnight.

The next day I took a shower and joined them at breakfast. The boy was called David.

He sat a distant from me, looking at me very carefully.

The breakfast was light, so I never at to my fill. The mother was not his real mother. David was German. He was adopted. So the couple had no children.

Lunch time. Again we sat at table in the same

places as we had done for breakfast. David sat a distance again. Fina-lly he asked the mother, *"**When are we going to paint him white?**"*

The Life-Jackets Picture

The End

THE FIRST THREE ELCR STUDENTS TO WIN
SCHOLARSHIPS: BIOs

A]: **Mushori Zhou** (ASPAU) Scholarship (1961)
AFRICAN
  SCHOLARSHIP PROGRAMME OF AMERICAN
    UNIVERSITIES.
1961 – *Admitted* at Missouri University, Missouri
State.
1965 – Graduated and returned home.
  • Back home he decided to pursue a
    Medical career.
1967 – Was admitted at *University of Rhodesia's*
Medical School
  • Qualified as a Medical Doctor (MD)
  • First posted at *Mpilo Hospital*, Bulawayo
  • Then, the war escalated
1976 – All Swedish Doctors were recalled home
leaving all Mission Hospitals empty; *Mnene,
Masase, Musume,*
  Manama
  • Took the risk and transferred to Mnene a
    virtual *war zone*
18 May 1977-Tragedy Struck- Inevitably was
brutally assassinated right in front of his official
Residence at *Mnene Hospital*.

B]: **Thomas Tlou** [LWF]: SCHOLARSHIP (1962)
Lutheran
world federation (Geneva)
1962 – Admitted at Luther College Decorah Iowa.

- Graduated with a Senior degree but did not
return home.
- Changed citizenship and adopted that of
Botswana
- Became eligible for Ambassadorial post of
his adopted country and was first
Ambassador of the UN.
- After his tour of duty, was appointed
Chancellor of Botswana University when
UBLS (University of Botswana, Lesotho,
and Swaziland) split and went their
separate ways.
- Thomas held that post until his retirement,
now late.

[C]: **Sifas Zhou** (dob-1939-) [ASPAU]:
SCHOLARSHIP (1962) AFRICAN
SCHOLARSHIP PROGRAMME OF
AMERICAN UNIVERSITIES

1962 - Admitted at *Wittenberg University* Springfield, Ohio.

1966 - Graduated and returned home.

1966-67 Taught at Manama and married *Sophia (née Nenkwa).*

1968-69 Transferred to Bernard Mizeki College.

1970-71 Taught at Chegato Secondary School

1972   Took Grad. CE at UR, [University of Rhodesia].

1973-75 Promoted and transferred to UCE as lecturer.

1976-80 Promoted and transferred to Mkoba Teachers'
College as senior lecturer

1978-80 Promoted to Vice Principal of Mkoba Teachers'
College

• Transferred to Ministry of Foreign Affairs

1980-86 Appointed Ambassador to Sweden at Independence, 1980.

• Extended to Norway, Denmark, and Finland.

• Lutheran World Service (Geneva)

1987-94 Appointed Director of Refugees based in Angola. Responsible for:

• Angolan Internal Displaced at Bita Camp
• SWAPO Refugees to 1990.
• ANC Refugees to 1994

1990-   Awarded an honorary Degree by *Wittenberg University Doctor of Humane Letters.*

Currently–A cattle rancher! *SHOKA FARM-GWANDA*

Made in the USA
Middletown, DE
12 March 2022

62514157R00040